MW00883975

How to
Study for the
USMLE™

Armin Kamyab, M.D.

authorHOUSE®

AuthorHouse™
1663 Liberty Drive, Suite 200
Bloomington, IN 47403
www.authorhouse.com
Phone: 1-800-839-8640

USMLE™ is a registered trademark of the Federation of State Medical Boards of the United States, Inc., and the National Board of Medical Examiners®, neither of which sponsors nor endorses this product.

First published by AuthorHouse 10/29/2008

Library of Congress Control Number: 2008908094

ISBN: 978-1-4389-0358-3 (e)
ISBN: 978-1-4389-0357-6 (sc)

Printed in the United States of America
Bloomington, Indiana

This book is printed on acid-free paper.

Table of Contents

Introduction

Whether you are a U.S. medical student, or an IMG, the most important exams of your medical career are the United States Medical Licensing Examinations. It is no surprise that so much money is spent on study materials, and so much time and effort is spent studying. Similarly, it is no surprise that so much fear comes from even the thought of taking the USMLEs.

Publishers, unfortunately, capitalize on this fear, which explains the immense volume of study materials available. Supply and demand; it is simple economics. Nervous and scared test-takers will spend money on whatever they feel will give them the upper hand.

Sure, there is irony in criticizing the mass volume of books aimed at helping you conquer the USMLEs, while contributing myself to the ever-growing list, so how is this book different?

Out of the hundreds of books out there relating to the USMLEs, most attempt to capture as much pertinent USMLE testable material as possible. They try to convince you that if you memorize all the information they present, then you will have a good chance of doing well. These books come in every shape and size. Some are point-form, whereas others are well-written texts. Some are short, and some are long. Some are good, and some are bad. Some come in fantastic, promising titles, such as "Ace the USMLE," or "Nail the boards."

Thus far, the only source I have found that adequately deals with the "how" of studying for the all-important USMLEs, is the first chapter of Kaplan®'s question book. As a result, it is unfortunate to see that there is an infinite amount of study material out there, but many test-takers simply do not know "how" to study. For this reason, and for the same reason that I wrote, *How to Study for Medical School*, I decided to write a book about *how* to study for the USMLE.

I can never stress this enough, but it is not simply a function of how long you study, how many textbooks you read, how you rank in your medical school class, or even your MCAT® score. The single most important factor that will affect your score is *how* you study, *how* you organize your study time, and also *how* you view the test.

Having studied and taken the USMLEs myself, I know that your time at this crucial period is of the essence, and the last thing you should be doing is reading a book that does not contain any test material! That being said, I have made every effort to present the material in a well-organized manner, with different chapters clearly outlining important test preparation topics, and written in an easy-to-read format.

So before plunging into that *First Aid*, make sure you spend a little bit of time reading this book, which will help you figure out *how* your next few weeks or months will be spent. A little goes a long way, and this could not be any truer than with USMLE preparation. Only with proper planning and preparation will you be able to conquer the USMLEs. Even though your time is valuable, having a solid study plan is even more valuable.

If you want to study more efficiently, be more organized, be more confident, and desire to do your best on the USMLE, then this book is for you.

* * *

This book was initially written for Step 1 preparation, but it can very well be applied towards Step 2CK and Step 3 preparation, as well for any other test.

Chapter 1

Know Where You Stand

Everyone likes to feel that they're somewhat prepared, but you really need to have a clear idea of where you stand. Are you sure you can recall all the branches of the thyrocervical trunk? Are you sure you remember the pathophysiology behind McCune-Albright syndrome? How about the mechanism of action of Baclofen? At this point, you are not trying to impress anyone, so be honest with yourself and be realistic in regards to your current knowledge base. If you are not, you will only limit your own success.

If you are a medical student nearing the end of the basic sciences, and you are starting to get ready to take the Step 1, then odds are you already have sound medical knowledge to build on. If you are a foreign graduate on the other hand, who has not reviewed the basic sciences since medical school ten years ago, then you most likely have forgotten many of the testable basic sciences details.

In either case, knowing where you stand will dictate how much time and effort you might need to spend studying. But be honest with yourself. Just because you finished the basic sciences in medical school last week, it does not mean that you have a strong foundation of the basic sciences! Wherever it is that you feel you stand, by admitting to yourself that you still have work to do, you are on the right track. And no matter where you stand, there is always room for improvement.

It is of course difficult to have a good idea of where you stand. I'm sure it has happened to many of you— where you felt very confident before a test, only to end up performing poorly. How can one overcome this dilemma and get a good idea of where one stands?

One very good way is to purchase one of the NBME practice tests (found on the self-assessment section of the NBME web site). There are a few different NBME practice tests available for purchase. Even if you take one now, there will still be other ones left to take as you get closer to taking your exam. You can find all the info you need regarding these NBME tests on their web site. If you take these tests in the timed mode, the score you receive is probably the best predictor of your USMLE score.

So take an NBME practice test as you begin to study for the USMLE, to have a realistic view of where you stand. It even gives you a performance profile, so that you know exactly which sections you are strong or weak in. The first NBME practice test I took right after completing the Basic Sciences gave me a score that was much lower than I had anticipated. It was quite an eye-opener, as I thought I would score a lot higher since the Basic Sciences were right behind me and I was fairly confident at the time. It made me realize just how much preparation I still had to do, not just in terms of the material, but also time management during the exam, staying calm, and building endurance for long exams.

Before going any further, the questions you should ask yourself at this time are:

- When did you last study the Basic Sciences? (if taking the Step 1)

- How did you do on an NBME practice exam?

- How confident do you feel with your knowledge base?

- How confident do you feel in your test-taking skills?

- Do you know what to expect on test day?

Once you know where you stand, you can create your schedule accordingly. In my case, for example, I knew that the knowledge-base was there, and I therefore knew I had to allocate more time to doing sample questions and less time for simply studying. This makes studying much more efficient, and will help you get the most out of your time spent preparing for this important exam.

It will also help you remain calm and confident throughout the period leading to the exam. You already know where you stand and what to expect. Therefore, you will not likely encounter any surprises down the road. You have already had time to come to grips with your current standings, and you are working on overcoming your weaknesses, while amplifying your strengths.

* * *

Knowing where you stand now will also provide a baseline from which you can monitor your progress. When you study for the USMLE, the progression curve is so gentle that you often do not notice that you are progressing, which can be extremely discouraging. However, having a baseline will show you just how much and how fast you are progressing—or worst case scenario, it will show you if you are not progressing!

To begin, let's assess your baseline standings. You should even write it all down from time to time, like a journal. The questions should be completely personalized, but some general questions you should answer every so often could be:

May 28 2006, Four weeks to go	
NBME score	226
How nervous are you about the test? (1-10)	6
What percentage of the material do you feel like you know?	80
How confident do you feel about your test-taking skills? (1-10)	7
What percentage do your Question-book scores average?	Mid 70s
What percentage do your online Question-bank scores average?	Low 70s

Whether you are treating a sick patient, working on paying your college loans, or studying for the USMLE, progress is ALWAYS good to see! It is a great way of staying motivated. You can also try to break the questions into subjects, such as, "How prepared do you feel in Anatomy on a scale of 1-10?" If you tend to have time management problems during tests, you can ask yourself questions such as, "On average, how many questions do you have remaining when the time runs out in a block?" Keep track of your improvements (or lack thereof), figure out where you need help, and where you are doing well.

CHAPTER 2.

Make A Plan

Now that you know where you stand, you can make a practical plan. What does that mean? It is quite simple; when you sit down to create a plan, consider the following questions.

- What is the USMLE?

- How is it structured?

- How can I do well on it?

- What book(s) should I be studying?

- Which practice questions should I be doing?

- How much time do I have until the exam?

- How much time each day am I realistically going to be studying?

What is the USMLE?

You will read different things about the USMLEs in different places, so I will just add one comment that I believe is warranted. The answers are concrete. It is as gray as black and white. Either you know the answer or you don't. This is not the verbal reasoning section of the MCAT®; this is important information that is actual, and learnable. There is nothing abstract or vague about it. It is based on science and on tangible material. Remember that when you are studying, every line you read could be a potential question.

Every comment I read about the USMLEs always seems to portray them as being some sort of absurd out-of-this-world examinations that are extremely difficult. In other words, they SCARE you. At this point, fear is not your friend, so isolate yourself from all negative comments regarding the USMLEs. Rather, embrace the exam—live it, and breathe it. Make it your best friend. Think about it first thing in the morning and last thing at night, rather than suppressing it out of fear. The USMLEs are very doable; you just have to spend the necessary time, and put the necessary effort into learning the material.

How is it structured?

Little will be said regarding the structure of the USMLE, since you can find this information on the USMLE web site. However, in terms of your plan, you need to know exactly how it is structured, so that you know exactly what to expect. In other words, know that is a computer-based test, know that it is eight hours long, know that it is divided into blocks, know how the breaks will work, know that it covers all basic sciences topics, and know that you do not receive your grade for three to four weeks after taking the test, etc.

Know as much as you can regarding the test (more on this in Chapter 11: Know Your Enemy). The more you know, the more mentally prepared you can be. You'll notice that knowing what to expect will take half the anxiety away.

How can I do well on it?

When you ask yourself, "How can I do well on it?" you are asking yourself what you need to focus on. Do you need to go back and review all the biochemical pathways, or do you need to sit down and practice doing blocks of fifty randomized questions in sixty minutes to sharpen your test-taking skills? This builds on what was mentioned in the first chapter, so make sure you know where you stand. Only by knowing where you are will you know where you can go. Begin by jotting notes about your strong areas as well as your weak areas. Tell yourself what you need to focus on. This will then come into play when you are setting up your study schedule (more on this in Chapter 4: Set up a Schedule).

What book(s) should I study, and which practice questions should I do? (Discussed further in Chapter 3: What Books Should I Be Using?)

How much time do I have until the exam?

How much time you have until the exam is highly variable for most people. Foreign graduates, for example, can give themselves months or even years if they want. U.S. graduates taking the Step 1, however, usually only have weeks, as it often needs to be passed before students can enter clinical rotations. This will affect the calendar you will set up in Chapter 4, but before we get to the scheduling part, figure out exactly how many weeks or months you are allocating to studying and preparing.

How much time each day am I realistically going to be studying?

How much time each day you are going to be studying is the part most will lie to themselves about. For example, even with the whole day off, I know that I will get at most only about three or four hours of solid studying accomplished in one day. Yes, even with the whole day off, just three or four hours of studying! Since I know that I will sleep in and wake up late, I might decide to cook (since I rarely have to time do it otherwise), I will go to the gym, I will watch TV, I will go out with friends, I might go shopping, and so on. That's fine, because I'm honest with myself, and I know that I will get at most four hours of studying done in a full day. I make my schedule accordingly to accommodate for it.

Be honest with yourself. It is better to do this than to convince yourself you'll be studying ten hours a day, and to make a schedule based on ten hours of studying each day, only to realize that you are realistically only accomplishing half of that. That will certainly get you into trouble.

* * *

You know where you stand, you know all about the exam, you know how much time you have until the exam, and you know how much time you will spend studying each day...

We now need to figure out what book(s) you will be using and what practice questions you will be doing.

CHAPTER 3.

What Books Should I Be Using?

There are hundreds of USMLE books out there, so how can you decide which books you should be reading? As with anything else, there are good ways of deciding which books to read, and there are bad ways. The following are the two best ways you could use to decide—browsing through books and asking seniors for advice.

Go to your local medical bookstore and browse through their books to see which ones you like, or which ones suit your learning style. For example, do you prefer a more point-form review book such as in First Aid, or more text and paragraphs such as in Crush? Books are expensive and after buying a few, the cost adds up. You want your purchases to be worthwhile, and to be something you will not mind reading and studying. There is nothing wrong with browsing through the books in order to figure out which work best for you.

Ask for suggestions from others who have already taken the test. This follows valuable advice my grade twelve English teacher used to always tell us, "Don't learn from your own mistakes; learn from someone else's mistakes." However, if you do ask seniors who have already taken the test, just make sure you don't ask one person, but rather ask around. Everyone is different, and a book that works for one person might not work for others. Therefore when you ask for advice from others, you want a general consensus. You want to use the books that EVERYONE boasts. You do not want to use that one book that only one person thought was useful while everyone else tells you to stay clear of it.

Similarly, when you ask seniors for advice, make sure you ask them how they did on their exam. It may sound inappropriate to ask, but believe me, someone who did well will be more than glad to share their score with you, and tell you how they did it. Clearly, you do not want advice from someone who just barely passed the exam! Hence, if someone doesn't want to reveal their score, take their advice with a grain of salt. The person may just be a private individual, but without knowing if the advice is coming from a reliable source, the advice may not be worth all that much.

That being said, do not just take their score into consideration, but also their drive and motivation.

Take the following two seniors, for example, both of whom took the exam:

- The one who got a score of 99 tells you, "Yeah, just read this one book, and you'll do fine. That's all I did!"

- The one who got a score of 215 tells you, "I really wanted to do well, so I asked seniors when I was in your shoes and followed all their recommendations. I read all of pathology from this book, reviewed physiology from this book, did online questions for anatomy from this web site, and they were all great sources."

Clearly, the latter senior was more dedicated to succeeding. He did his research in finding good study material when he was in your shoes. His score might have been due to nervousness during the test, or perhaps the random nature of the test may have been biased towards a subject that he was particularly weak in. Regardless of the score, the latter senior's advice is much more useful.

* * *

There are two other commonly used bad ways of deciding which books you should use. The first one, which I see all the time, is taking advice from others who have not yet taken the test. A lot of people like to pretend that they know what they're doing, and want it to appear to their colleagues as if they're on

Armin Kamyab, M.D.

the ball. Clearly, their advice only takes you so far, as they have no way of really knowing if the books they're using for exam preparation are good or not.

The second, commonly used, but poor way of choosing your study materials is buying books based on online bookstore customer reviews. This one might have been a shocker to some of you, but in case you have not noticed, a lot of the customer reviews you find on popular online bookstores might not be real customer reviews, but rather reviews from friends or family members of the author (or possibly from the author him/herself). So be weary of the hundreds of USMLE books out there. Many are not very good despite the "five star" ratings and excellent customer reviews! Stick to books that have been tried, tested and true.

* * *

The same principals above apply when deciding which practice questions to do; be sure to take advice from seniors who have done well. You do not want to be that first buyer of a brand new question book you found online. Let others try it out first. Your time is valuable, so use it wisely. Stick to books and question sources that have already been proven effective.

That being said, you should never run out of questions to do. Generally speaking, any practice question you do is a good question. Just because you ran out of questions to do based on recommendations from friends/colleagues, is no excuse to stop doing questions or to redo the same questions. There are hundreds of question books available, and even if you may not know which ones are good and which are bad, just pick one of them and do the questions.

Ultimately, compared to not doing any questions, there is really no such thing as "bad" questions for study purposes.

* * *

Review books or textbooks?

Many who prepare for the USMLE contemplate this pertinent question. Should you read Robbins *Pathologic Basis of Disease* or *BRS pathology*? Should you read *First Aid's* physiology section, or Guyton's *Textbook of Medical Physiology*?

There is no clear-cut answer, but the following is one method of helping you get the most out of your valuable study time, and it is the successful method I used for all USMLEs.

- Use one main review book that covers all subjects

- Use many reference textbooks

- Use a big textbook for your one or two

 weakest subjects

The review book is where you should focus most of your studying around, as it will ensure that you cover all the basics, in all the subjects. It will give you a great, broad foundation, and you should even be able to pass the exam by just studying any of the popular review books.

By the nature of their description, however, review books are condensed and not as detailed as you would like for that ninety-nine. That's why you also need reference books from time to time to look up things that are either not in the review books or not covered in enough detail. Nowadays, keep in mind that you can also look up everything online, and you might not even need reference textbooks!

Everyone has that one subject or two that they're just weak in, or possibly an organ system that just doesn't commit to memory. For example, when I was studying for the Step 1, for some reason, pulmonary pathology would always stump me no matter how many times I read review books or small reference textbooks. It would consistently be my worst section of any practice test I would do. So I read the whole chapter in big Robbins on pulmonary pathology, line per line (of course making notes while reading, Chapter 5: Study Efficiently). I hated doing it, it was grueling, it took me almost a week to do it, and it was full of useless detailed information otherwise reserved for pathologists, but lo and behold, pulmonary pathology was no longer my weakest area.

Figure out what your absolute worst subject is, and spend the extra time reading a detailed, reliable textbook on it even if it takes a few days out of your already-busy schedule. Maybe it's just me (and probably entirely psychological), but don't exams always seem to focus on your weak areas?

* * *

Now that you know which books you will be using and which questions you will be doing, you are ready to create a schedule.

CHAPTER 4.

Set Up a Schedule

By now you know what kind of exam you are dealing with, and you have an idea of what you need to do in order to succeed. You now need to come up with a schedule. This is the most labor-intensive part of the preparatory phase, but it is also the most important. You simply cannot study without a concrete day-to-day study schedule to go by.

There are a lot of things to consider when making a schedule.

- Schedule around work/school

- Cover every subject

- Randomize

- Include review time

- Include blocks for doing questions

- Include catch-up dates

- The last week

Schedule around work/school

This one is pretty self-explanatory. There should never be any excuses for not studying simply because you work or are currently in school. You simply need to take it into consideration and schedule around it.

Cover every subject

Be sure to cover every subject that is covered on the USMLE, and be sure to allocate the right amount of time to each. You do not want to study pathology for only two hours a week, while you schedule five hours a week for epidemiology! Prioritize, not only in terms of which topics are mostly likely to be tested, but also in terms of which topics YOU need to spend the most time on. This goes back to what we discussed in Chapter 1, Know Where You Stand.

If you have no idea which topics you need to spend more time on, then this is where it helps to have taken a sample NBME practice test. The performance profile that is given should help guide your study schedule, and help you decide how much time you should spend for each subject. I remember from my first performance profile, respiratory was one of my worst sections. I therefore allocated a good 20 to

30 percent of my week to just studying respiratory physiology and respiratory pathology.

Although you ultimately want to cover everything, you clearly want to spend a little more time every week on topics you are weak in. Do not completely neglect subjects you shine in, however, because even though you might excel in it now, all that knowledge may not necessarily stay fresh in your mind in the weeks to come. No matter how confident you are in any of the subjects, keep reviewing them, even if it is for only a few hours per week.

Randomize

You need to randomize your schedule, just like the exam. You are always told that the best way to do practice questions is to randomize the question blocks, right? Studying is no different. You want your brain to get accustomed to switching from topic to topic. For example, cover one topic in the morning, a different topic in the afternoon, and a different topic in the evening.

This way you spread the material out, and cover all the subjects more consistently, as opposed to doing physiology for three days followed by microbiology for two days, and then pathology for four days.

A student once told me she hated switching from topic to topic when she studied, and could only study if she stayed with one subject for a few days, finished it, and then moved on. It made more sense to her this way. The only question I ask is that if you cannot handle switching from subject to subject in the comfort of your own study space, at your own leisurely time, how do you expect to be able to do it every minute during the exam?

Another downfall to studying the subjects in large blocks is that after you have covered every subject, odds are you forgot most of what you learned in the first subject you studied. By spreading it out, and doing, for example, a little physiology today, and little physiology in a few days, then every time you study it, you will review and build on things you read the previous times. You may also run into certain familiar topics or terms, and ask yourself, "What was that again?" You will then go back and quickly browse through your notes and refresh your mind. You would basically be combining studying and reviewing, and hence much more efficient use of your preparation time.

This method of review is especially true in pathology where there are a lot of associations. For example, when you are studying renal pathology and read about Wegener's Granulomatosis, in a few weeks when you read pulmonary pathology and encounter Wegener's Granulomatosis again, the term will sound familiar to you, but you may have forgotten what it is. So you go back through your renal notes to find it, and you review that section again.

Similarly, you can often have associations between different subjects. Sticking with renal pathology, you will read about Glomerulosclerosis. In a few weeks when you are studying microbiology, you will encounter this term again when you are reading about Hepatitis C or HIV. Rather than just memorizing in microbiology that Hepatitis C and HIV are associated with Glomerulosclerosis, go back to your renal pathology notes and re-read Glomerulosclerosis. This way if the question is a microbiology question, but presented from a pathology point of view, you will be set.

Spreading out the subjects makes your study time much more efficient, and will train your brain to think the way the USMLE wants you to think; being able to jump from subject to subject, and being able to associate topics within a subject, or between different subjects (more on associations and cross-references in Chapter 8: How To Review).

Include review time

This is in reference to reviewing your notes (taking notes is discussed in Chapter 5: Study More Efficiently).

After looking at my schedule, you may have noticed no doubt that I always leave time for "reviewing." It is absolutely crucial to reflect on what you have read and to review the notes you have taken. The best ways of doing so are to spend an hour or two every single night reflecting on what you studied that day and read notes that you took that day, as well as spending time every weekend reviewing notes taken during that week.

Notice how taking notes has a great advantage of making your review time more efficient. You spent the entire day going through twenty to thirty pages of a textbook or review book, but at night, you need only spend an hour going over five pages of your condensed notes, which covers the pertinent material presented in those twenty to thirty pages. Remember to take notes from everything you study, whether it is textbooks, review books, or even video and audio files!

Reviewing often will also ensure constant exposure to the material. In addition, it will simplify and facilitate future reviewing, since you are constantly updating your notes, adding things you think are important, removing things you already know, cross-referencing things, etc. (more on reviewing and updating your notes in Chapter 8: How To Review). Every time you review, your notes become more complete and more resourceful, while you simultaneously absorb more of the pertinent information.

Include blocks for doing questions

Doing practice questions is discussed further in Chapter 6 (How To Use Questions As Study Tools), but in regards to the schedule you are setting up, you need to incorporate questions into your schedule and you need to incorporate a lot of them. Practice doing questions and sharpen your test-taking skills because it is in some ways even more important than studying the material itself. Colleagues of mine who scored 250 and above on the USMLEs were not all the brightest students or the most disciplined. Some were just superb test-takers. Do not neglect the importance of practicing your questions, and leave yourself ample time each week to doing questions.

How much time to allocate each week for questions depends on how much time you have until the exam. If you notice, my "early" schedule has time allotted for online question banks maybe once or twice per week (Schedule A at the end of this chapter). My "later" schedules, in contrast, have time allotted for online question banks maybe four or five times per week (Schedule C at the end of this chapter). Again, the reason is simple—you need to first learn the material, and then start sharpening your test-taking skills as you get closer to your exam date.

Scheduling time for doing questions this way can be a little tricky, but just try to schedule it progressively. For example, if you are giving yourself six weeks to study:

- During the first two weeks, do online questions two days per week

- During the middle two weeks, do online questions four days per week

- During the last two weeks, do online questions five or six days per week

This way you are progressively getting accustomed to doing more and more questions, and you will have an easier time getting used to it. Another way of doing this is:

- The week before the exam, leave yourself one non-question day per week

- Two weeks before the exam, leave yourself two non-question days per week

- Three weeks before the exam, leave yourself three non-question days per week

- And so on...

Just be sure to start your USMLE prep by focusing on learning the material first and foremost. You will get a lot more out of the practice questions if you have a solid foundation of the material being tested.

Beginning of your prep: Closer to exam date:

S T U D Y   **study**

questions   **QUESTIONS**

Lastly, regarding scheduling time for questions, if you look at my schedule, you will notice that time allotted to doing online question banks are all in the morning. The reason for this is simple: the USMLEs are on a computer and are all in the morning. You want to start getting accustomed to answering questions on the computer in the morning. For the same reason, I didn't schedule any time for practicing questions from question books in the morning, because answering questions from a printed book is not representative of the actual exam, and hence no added benefit is gained from practicing questions from question books in the morning. So try as much as possible to allocate mornings to doing practice question on the computer.

Include catch-up days

You managed to set up a schedule, which includes all topics, with time for review, and time for questions. What happens if something unexpected comes up and you fall behind? And believe me, something always comes up! It could be a friend's party, a family event, your favorite movie being shown on TV, or a friend on the phone who talks for hours.

This is why you need to schedule time for catching-up, and you will notice that in the sample schedules at the end of this chapter. Every other week or so, leave yourself a weeknight, and/or half a weekend completely free, to use for catch-up, if need be. You have nothing to lose by doing this, and everything to gain. If you fall behind, you'll have some cushion to fall back on. If you're up to date, then that's fantastic! Use this extra time to your advantage and either start getting ahead in your studies, do practice questions, or better yet, just relax and take a well-deserved break!

The last week

At this point, you should start easing up on questions. You should not be studying anything at all, and you should spend most of your time reviewing your notes.

Even if you have not finished all the questions in a question bank that you purchased, it's okay. It is better to go back and review what you have already studied than to try to move on and learn new material without completely having memorized everything to date. One of the worst feelings is that of running into a question during the exam that covers material you know you've covered, but you just cannot recall it, because you did not review it sufficiently.

That last week, put off learning new things. Accept the fact that it's over, and that you did all you could to date. Focus instead on memorizing everything else you covered in the last weeks/months, and put most of your focus and energy on reviewing your notes (both your notes from books as well as those from the questions you did).

Everyone has those few things that they always forget, no matter how many times they review. For me, they were the developmental milestones, the inborn errors of metabolism, and the congenital immunodeficiency disorders. Make a few pages of notes—one for each topic you constantly have problems retaining—and the last week make sure you go over these pages every day, including the morning of the exam. Since you have a hard time learning these few things that always seem to slip your mind, then at least you should try relying on short-term recall!

* * *

The following are three samples from schedules that I used during Step 1 and Step 2 preparation:

A—The first table is a sample from my Step 1 study schedule, in the early weeks of my preparation.

B—The second table is a sample from my Step 2 study schedule during clinical rotations (notice how you can use this schedule to accommodate for work or lectures as well).

C—The third table is a sample from my Step 1 study schedule, in the weeks closer to my Step 1 date (though the general idea of incorporating more questions as I got closer to the exam date was also used for my Step 2 schedule).

Schedule A. The Early Weeks of Preparation

Week of Sunday May 6

Sunday May 6	Monday	Tuesday	Wednesday	Thursday	Friday	Saturday
Online Question Bank	Read First Aid® Biochemistry	Finish First Aid® Biochemistry section	Online Question Bank	Read High-Yield Neuro	Read Robbin's® Pathology Pulmonary section	CATCH UP!
Read First Aid® Pharmacology	Read First Aid® Cardiology	Kaplan® Qbook 1 block	Finish taking note from questions	Kaplan® Qbook 1 block	Kaplan® Qbook 1 block	Question Book ONLY IF Caught up
		type notes	Read First Aid® Biochemistry			Read First Aid® Physiology
Finish taking notes from QBank	Review notes Taken today		Review notes From today	Finish taking notes from Qbook	Finish taking notes from Qbook	Finish taking Notes from Qbook
Relax!		9p House on TV!				

Week of Sunday May 13

Sunday May 13	Monday	Tuesday	Wednesday	Thursday	Friday	Saturday
Online Question Bank	Finish reading Robin's Pulmonary section	Read High-Yield Embryology	Listen to Audio files... (don't forget to take notes)	Audio files... (don't forget to take notes)	Audio files... (don't forget to take notes)	CATCH UP!
First Aid® Microbiology	Read First Aid® G.I.	Kaplan® Qbook 1 block	Read First Aid® Neuro and Anatomy	Kaplan® Qbook 1 block	CATCH UP!	Question Book ONLY IF caught up
						Read First Aid® Pathology
Finish taking notes from QBank	Review notes taken while study	type notes from Qbook	Review notes taken while study	Review notes taken while study	Review notes From the week!	Review notes from today

Schedule B. Studying During Clinical Rotations

Sunday May 6	Monday	Tuesday	Wednesday	Thursday	Friday	Saturday
Online Question Bank	WORK/ SCHOOL	WORK/ SCHOOL	WORK/ SCHOOL	WORK/ SCHOOL	WORK/ SCHOOL	CATCH UP
Read First Aid® Pharmacology	Read First Aid® Cardiology	Kaplan® Qbook 1 block	Read First Aid® Biochemistry	Read First Aid® Physiology	Read High-Yield Neuro	QBook® ONLY IF Caught up
Finish taking notes for the day	Review notes taken today	Finish typing notes from Qbook 9p House on TV!	Review notes from today	Review notes from today	Review notes from today	Review notes from the week
Relax!						

Sunday May 13	Monday	Tuesday	Wednesday	Thursday	Friday	Saturday
Online Question Bank	WORK/ SCHOOL	WORK/ SCHOOL	WORK/ SCHOOL	WORK/ SCHOOL	WORK/ SCHOOL	CATCH UP
First Aid® Microbiology	Read First Aid® G.I.	Kaplan® Qbook 1 block	Read First Aid® Neuro and Anatomy	CATCH-UP (If caught-up, Review First Aid® Microbiology)	**Review First Aid®** Pharmacology	QBook **ONLY IF caught up**
Finish taking notes for the day	Review notes from today	type notes from today	Review notes from today		Review notes from the week	Read First Aid® Pathology
						Catch up and/or review notes from the week

Schedule C. The Weeks Closer to Exam Date

Sunday May 6	Monday	Tuesday	Wednesday	Thursday	Friday	Saturday
Online Question Bank 1 block	Online Question Bank 2 blocks back-to-back	Review your Biochemistry notes	Online Question Bank 2 blocks back-to-back	Online Question Bank 2 blocks back-to-back	Review your Pathology notes	CATCH UP!
Review your Pharmacology notes	Review your Cardiology notes	Question Book 1 block	Review your Physiology notes	Review your Histology notes	Question Book 1 block	Question Book ONLY IF caught up
Finish taking notes from QBank	Review notes of your choice	9p House on TV!	Review notes of your choice	Review notes of your choice	Review notes of your choice	Review Your Notes
Relax!						

Sunday May 13	Monday	Tuesday	Wednesday	Thursday	Friday	Saturday
Online Question Bank 1 block	Reviewing Your Pathology notes	Review your Embryology and Anatomy notes	Online Question Bank 2 blocks back-to-back	Review your Microbiology notes	Online Question Bank 2 blocks back-to-back	CATCH UP!
Review Your Notes	Review your G.I. notes	Question Book 1 block	Review your Neuro notes	Question Book 1 block	CATCH UP!	Question Book ONLY IF caught up
	Review notes of your choice	Review notes of your choice	Review notes of your choice	Review notes of your choice	Review notes of your choice!	Review Immunology notes
						Review notes of your choice

CHAPTER 5.

Study Efficiently

It's not good enough to just study. How you study is crucial. As I always like to say, it's not quantity, but quality. The most important thing you need to do when you study is to take notes.

If any of you have read my first book, then you understand how important it is to take notes. Nonetheless, I will dwell into this to some extent again. Please read the following excerpt from my previous book, titled How to Study in Medical School.

"Chapter 1. Take Notes.

When you take notes, you study actively. Many of us can attest to times when we are reading, only to abruptly wake up from a daydream and ask ourselves, "What did I just read?" Taking notes as you are studying forces you to be more attentive, because you are not only reading, but you are also deciding which parts of what you are reading are important. You actively decide which parts are not important, which sections are likely to be asked on tests, which parts you can skip, and so on. Right away, your attention level has gone up drastically.

After you have read your books and know what you need to write in your notes, you now have to physically write/type your notes. Once again, you are forced to pay attention, because unlike reading, writing requires a lot more attentiveness and alertness. You may doze off from time to time while reading, but since you are constantly reading and then writing notes, your chances of dozing off are lower. Writing requires a higher level of baseline cerebral functioning than reading, where you often end up just staring at words.

Taking notes is in no way a shortcut. It is actually an attempt to know everything! The purpose is not to condense or summarize, but to analyze, re-organize, research, and remove all the filler that is in lecture notes and textbooks."

I have left some parts out, but the message is clear. By taking notes, you will study more actively, you will retain more as you study, and you will condense what you are reading for future review.

It might feel funny taking notes and condensing 'review books,' because by definition these books are already meant to be "high yield" and are meant to only present pertinent information, right? There is one big problem, and to discuss it let's take the *First Aid* for example. You cover one chapter, for example, the cardiology chapter. Now how much have you retained? Did you memorize every word you just read?

Even though you probably should have, you likely did not. Perhaps you assume you will read the chapter again at some future date, or worse yet, you hope that during the USMLE the answer will just "come to you," because you think you covered the material. In reality, you almost certainly will not have time to come back and read those chapters again, and the answer will most definitely not come to you just by having read the chapter once. You truly need to understand and memorize the material, and you have to try to do so the first time around.

Clearly, no one can memorize everything after a first read, even by actively studying and taking notes. So here is where the condensing part comes into play. By taking notes, there are certain things you can leave out, and the reason is because review books try very hard to cover EVERYTHING. So when you read the cardiology chapter, there is a lot of information there that you already know, and that you know you will remember in the weeks to come. Hence if you do not take notes and come back one day to re-read the chapter, you have no choice but to re-read the WHOLE chapter, including material you already know. This wastes valuable study time. When you take notes, however, you can omit material that you are already familiar with, and that you know you will remember in the weeks to come. By doing so, you can convert a twenty-page *First Aid* chapter into ten pages or less.

Do you realize that you just cut your future study time by half? Even if you do feel you need to cover cardiology again in the future, instead of having to spend six hours reading the whole *First Aid* chapter again, which includes redundant information, you just need to spend three hours reviewing your notes, which only cover pertinent material that you may have forgotten.

* * *

While studying for my Step 1, I had condensed the whole *First Aid* into twenty-seven pages of notes. Those twenty-seven pages contained only information that I knew I would forget a few weeks after reading the *First Aid*. So the days before my test, instead of wasting time going through a whole review book and reading unnecessary information, I only reviewed my notes, which gave me the essential information I needed and only the essential information.

It is crucial to start taking notes early. You need to start the first time you open your review book. This will drastically increase your efficiently, because every time you review after that, you can simply read your notes instead.

CHAPTER 6.

How to Use Questions as Study Tools

You may not realize it, but most of you will end up doing (at the very least) somewhere around 3,000 to 4,000 practice questions. That's a lot of questions! The unfortunate part is that the day of the test, odds are you will not remember more than half of the questions you did, or the important topics that were being relayed in those questions. There is a way around this though, to help you retain information contained in the questions you did, and it builds on something that was covered in the previous chapter—take notes.

Taking notes is not just for when you are reading books and studying, but it also applies to when you do questions. No matter how you score on a block of questions, and how confident you feel about your abilities to answer the questions, always read the explanations in full and always take notes of material that you feel is vital. No matter how confident you feel now, in a few weeks or months you might not remember something that you know now.

This could not be any truer than with the recent trend that I have been noticing of studying material that you just studied, or doing subject-specific question blocks. For example, studying microbiology on Monday, and doing practice microbiology questions on Tuesday. I cannot stress how inefficient this is, and how it gives a false sense of security. It is one of the worst things that you can do in terms of studying. Clearly, if you studied microbiology on Monday, and you do microbiology questions on Tuesday, odds are you will score fairly well on the question blocks, and you will feel like you know what you need to know! Wrong.

Always randomize the question blocks. If you choose to do subject-specific blocks, then at least do them many weeks after studying that subject. It will benefit you in two ways:

1.   You will find out if you truly know the material, as opposed to just relying on short-term memory.

2.   You can consider it as another day of going over that subject. For example, studying biochemistry now, and doing biochemistry questions in three weeks. When you do the biochemistry questions and read the explanations in three weeks, it can be considered another day of studying biochemistry. You will learn new things, and more importantly,

you will go over things you forgot since the last three weeks.

Lastly, regarding taking notes, when you do questions, keep in mind that you most certainly will not have time to go back and re-do 3,000 questions, or go back and re-read all the explanations, but you definitely should have time during the weeks leading up to the test to read forty pages of your notes, which contain all the important information presented in those 3,000 questions.

* * *

Those big online question banks know what topics are important; it is their business to do so. It is why they are still in business, and it is why people keep subscribing to them. Therefore when you do their question banks, it is not enough to just do the questions, read the explanations, and then move on thinking you have retained everything (or worse, thinking that the same question will be asked again). The questions are deeper than that.

You need to thoroughly understand and memorize the information that is being presented in the explanations. It is not just a matter of knowing what the right answer is, but more importantly, why the wrong answers are wrong. Let me assure you that the questions asked on the USMLE will seldom ever be the same as those found in question banks. The USMLE wants to make sure you have understood and memorized certain important topics, and not just memorized other questions! Similarly, question banks are developed to ensure that you understand certain objectives. They are not meat for you to simply know what the correct answer is to a certain question.

Spend the time when you do practice questions. Use them as a study tool. Spend as much time on a block as you would reading a textbook chapter. It is not atypical to spend two or three hours on a block of questions, reading all the explanations in full and taking notes. It should take you an hour or two just to go over the explanations, and perhaps another hour to take notes. This is perfectly normal, and you will be plenty glad you did this closer to your exam date when you are reviewing your notes.

CHAPTER 7.

Sample Notes

The following are samples from my Step 1 and Step 2 notes, which were taken from textbooks, review books, question explanations, and any other relevant source that I came across. They were typed and put in point-form format, although any note taking style of your choosing is a good one. You will be reviewing them, so make sure to write/type your notes in a format that you will want to review.

You will notice that at times, the topics are completely randomized (as discussed in the "Randomize" section of Chapter 5: Set up a Schedule). Remember that this makes your review more effective for test-taking purposes, because you are training your brain to get accustomed to switching from topic to topic, just as the exam does. You are expected to be able to switch from one subject matter to another every minute during the exam—for eight long hours. Start getting used to it.

In each of the sample notes, you will also notice features mentioned in Chapter 8 (How to Review), such as **bolding**, <u>underlining</u>, making references to facts previously encountered, etc. Again, your notes are for you. Do as you wish with them. Modify them in any way you see fit.

Step 1 Sample Notes

-Von-Hippel Lindau (Chromosome 3) is a deletion of the VHL gene (a tumor suppressor). Need to know that apart from bilateral renal cell carcinoma, we can also get hemangioblastoma of the retina/cerebellum/medulla

-HGPRT converts Guanine to GMP, AND Hypoxanthine to Inosine

-IGF's and Insulin act on Tyr Kinase receptors

-With cerebellar ataxia, you fall even with eyes open.
-With sensory ataxia, you don't fall with eyes open, because you can use vision for sensory cues, but fall when close your eyes (because the problem is you can't 'feel' where your feet are)

-The parasite Strongyloides Stercoralis stays in once it gets in, so it's not found in stool samples.

-Smell is dealt with by the Pyriform cortex

-Collagen 4 of BM's is made by the basement membrane
-Collagen 1 is made by fibroblasts

-Primidone's metabolites are Phenobarb and PEMA

-Laron Dwarfism is due to absence of GH-Receptors

-Bony overgrowth like in Osteopetrosis decreases the BM cavity size, hence possibly causing pancytopenia

-With Meconium Ileus, don't forget to consider Cystic-Fibrosis

-A Thyrotoxic crisis commonly occurs with Grave's, and is trigged by stressors such as infection, trauma, childbirth, or even radio-iodine treatment.

-'Palisading nuclei' is found in Basal cell carcinoma

-Thick filaments of muscles (made up of myosin 2 heavy & 4 light) anchor to the Z-disks via Titin
-Thin filaments (F-actin) anchor via α-actinin

-Retrograde movement in neurons is done via dynein, and is **SLOW**

-The blood supply to the Pars Nervosa (aka the posterior pituitary) is the Inferior Hypophyseal artery

-hCG is secreted by **Syncytiotrophoblasts**

-Iron inhibits 5-Ala Synthase (2nd enzyme of heme synthesis) & Ferrochelatase (last enzyme)

-Leptin is produced by white adipocytes in response to nutritional intake, to induce utilization of carbs and lipids. It acts on the hypothalamus to inhibit overfeeding, by inhibiting the release of Neuropeptide Y.
-If there's something wrong with Leptin receptors, will therefore get obese and get Diabetes Mellitus (because you overeat, and can't utilize carbs and lipids)

-Blood glucose can be maintained by glycogen for 10-18 hours (after that, liver glycogen is exhausted, and the liver activates gluconeogenesis to maintain blood glucose)

-Rapid breakdown of muscle occurs within the first few days of starvation
-After several days of starvation though, it's Fatty Acids that supply Ketone Bodies...this is so that under prolonged starvation, we spare our muscles.

-Arginine is the only non-essential amino acids that's essential in children (it's made from Glutamate in the Urea cycle, and this pathway can meet the needs of an adult, but NOT that of a growing child)

-The Cloacal membrane is only made up of 2 layers (endoderm and ectoderm)

-The ligamentum teres and the ligamentum venosum separate the left lateral and the left medial segments of the liver.

-Brunner's glands are seen in the submucosa of the Duodenum (secrete alkaline substance to buffer the chyme)

-Receptive relaxation of the stomach is a vagovagal reflex (both afferent and efferent are CN10)

-Linea semilunaris is the area lateral to the abdominal recti muscles, where the aponeuroses of the internal oblique and the transverse fuse. (hence a vertical line on either side of the rectus abdominis muscles)

-Juxtamedullary nephrons (~20%) have loops of Henle in the Medulla
-Cortical nephrons (~80%) do not have loops of Henle...hence play no role in concentrating the urine

-Renal genesis requires the joining of the metanephric bud with the Ureteric bud (this is what later becomes the DCT & CT)

-Mullerian inhibiting substance is released by Sertoli cells

-Cricothyroid is supplied by the **External Laryngeal n**.

-Arenavirus is the ONLY virus that carries Ribosome with it! (Acquired from the host)

-In the cavernous sinus, CN6 is the thing that's closest to the internal carotid a.

-The Greater Petrosal n. is for Lacrimation

-H&E stains everything pink/red except for the nucleus, nucleoli, and calcium. (these become blue/purple)

-Alcaptonuria is excretion of Homogentisic acid (alkapton) in the urine due to congenital lack of the enzyme homogentisate (urine becomes dark, skin and stool also become dark).

-In low ATP states (like with ischemia), the cell decreases protein synthesis, but increases glycolysis.

-Coin lesions in periphery of lungs, think adenocarcinoma or bronchoalveolar carcinoma (of which adenocarcinoma is more strongly associated with smoking)

-Charcot-Bouchard aneurysms are small parenchymal hemorrhages associated with Hypertension

-We see dome-shaped urothelial cells in the outer-most cell layer of cysticercosis

-Tendon pains, think side-effect of **Quinolones** (don't forget Nalidixic acid is a quinolone)
-Seizures/neuropathies, think side-effect of Metronidazole

-Stanford Binet test only assesses verbal skills

-Post-infection encephalomyelitis is common with many viruses (measles, varicella, rubella, mumps, influenza, and their vaccines). We see here perivenous microglial involvement, and demyelination

-De-myelination of white matter in brain and abnormal giant Oligodendrocytes, think Progressive Multifocal Leukoencephalopathy.

-IL-4 is for IgE
-IL-5 is for IgA

-By definition, granuloma will have epithelioid macrophages/histiocytes (So multinucleated giant cells with asteroid bodies in them can be seen)

-**VEGF** mRNA expression is increased in muscle even just an hour into exercise!

-Exercise decreases Myoglobin O_2 saturation, as well as Intracellular O2 (because you're using it up!)

-BP falls by ~50 in arterioles, and by ~20 in capillaries (so arterioles cause the greatest decrease in BP)

-In Klinefelter's, we do have hyperplastic Leydig cells, but they're not functional.

-Parvo-B19 (slapped cheeks/5th disease), can cause Rheumatoid-like bilateral arthralgias and arthritis

-**Lewy bodies** are Eosinophilic (Lewy body is associated mainly with Parkinson's)

-Too much O_2 in a baby can affect the Retina, because of an inappropriate vascular proliferation (leading to exudation, hemorrhage, and eventually detachment of the retina)

-Only 2% of Hydatidiform moles progress to Choriocarcinoma

-Klumpke's was due to outstretched **arm**s
-Erb's head was bent **B**ack

-Anterior ½ of external ear canal → Auriculo-temporal n.
-Posterior ½ of external ear canal → Auricular branch of vagus n.
-Lower part of Auricle → Greater Auricular n.
-Upper part of Auricle → Lesser Occipital n.

-Amyloid AA (acute phase protein) is produced by Liver during inflammatory reactions (like RA or chronic infections)
-Amyloid AL (light chain) is an Ig (so look for it in Myelomas, or B-cell lymphomas...etc)

-Chorda Tympani n. carries taste to anterior 2/3 of tongue (recall CN 7), as well as stimulation for Sublingual and Submandibular glands (recall also CN 7)

-Tip of tongue drains to submental nodes, body of tongue drains to deep cervical

-Facial vein drains to Pterygoid venous plexus, then to emissary vein, then to cavernous sinus (hence how a pimple can infect the CNS)

-The Semilunar ganglion is for CN5

-Foramen Rotundum is for CN V2
-Forman Ovale is for CN V3
-Superior Orbital Fissure is for CN's 3, 4, 6, V1, and the opthalmic vein

Step 2 Sample Note'

-Newborns can have RBC's, elevated leukocytes, and elevated protein in the <u>CSF</u>

-In <u>Henoch-Schönlein purpura</u> (aka Anaphylactoid Purpura), platelets/coagulation are NORMAL! The purpura are caused by IgA's! (and not thrombocytopenia or anything like that)

-<u>Berger/IgA nephropathy</u> just causes IgA-mediated nephropathy (usually following URTI*).
-<u>Henoch-Schönlein purpura</u> causes IgA-mediated nephropathy, palpable purpura, arthralgia, and abdominal pain (also orchitis, scrotal edema, and intussusception!).
(*differentiate IgA nephro with post-strep in that post-strep has **decreased C3**!)

-Brown recluse spider bite is localized and delayed (Black Widow spider systemic and sudden).
(Treat the localized necrosis of brown widow with **Dapsone**)

-In <u>Familial Dysautonomia</u> (aka "<u>Riley-Day Syndrome</u>"), we see no tears, decreased pain sensation, smooth tongue (no taste buds), difficulty swallowing (hence aspiration/lung infections), GI dysmotility, episodic hypertension/orthostatic hypotension.

-<u>Deaf albino</u>, think <u>Tietz syndrome</u>. (<u>Tietze's syndrome</u> is costochondritis).

-Down-slanting eyes, webbed neck, low ears, pulmonary stenosis, cryptorchidism, lax joints, short, chest deformity, mental retardation, bleeding diathesis, think <u>Noonan Syndrome</u>.

-<u>Erysipelas</u> (**Strep, Pen/Macrolid**), think sharply demarcated. 'Can' block lymphatics, hence causing red streaking. Differentiate from Cellulitis by its raised advancing edges and sharp borders.

-<u>Brugada Syndrome</u> (A-D), abnormal EKG and increased risk of sudden death (via V. Fib). Most common cause of sudden death in young healthy men in South-East Asia.

-<u>Erythema Nodosum</u> is an inflammation of the fat cells under the skin (panniculitis). It causes <u>painful</u>, red nodules that are usually seen on the shins. It's an <u>immunologic response</u> to a variety of things.
(This is common in Sarcoidosis, hypersensitivity to drugs, infections, RF, or IBD)
(This can cause a False-Positive VDRL!)

-<u>Sarcoidosis</u> with <u>erythema nodosum</u>, <u>hilar lymphadenopathy</u>, and <u>arthralgia</u>, is called "<u>Lofgren Syndrome</u>".
-<u>Sarcoidosis</u> with <u>anterior uveitis</u>, <u>parotitis</u>, <u>CN7 palsy</u> and <u>fever</u> is called "<u>Heerfordt-Waldenstrom Syndrome</u>".

-Non-immune hydrops, macerated skin, thrombocytopenia...think **Early** <u>congenital</u> <u>syphilis</u>.
-Hutchinson teeth, mulberry molars, saber shins, CN8 problems...think **Late** <u>congenital</u> <u>syphilis</u>.

-With <u>Internal os open</u>, think either <u>inevitable abortion</u>, <u>incomplete abortion</u> (in both cases, do emergency D&C).
-In <u>septic abortion</u>, apart from antibiotics and cervical/blood cultures, also do <u>(gentle)</u> <u>suction curettage/evacuation</u> (to get rid of the left-over dead infected fetus).
-For a fetus >16 weeks, have to induce labor and evacuate uterus to avoid DIC.
-For <u>threatened abortion</u>...do pelvic rest and abstinence from sex and heavy activities.
(*don't forget about RhoGAM in all Rh(-) who are bleeding!)

-Crack/cocaine effect on the heart & lungs include vasospasms, pulm fibrosis, perforation of septum.
(Treat crack/cocaine intoxication with Benzo, NTG, and ASA. Avoid B-blockers cuz will increase effect on alpha-receptors)

-<u>Infant botulinum</u> is caused by <u>ingesting the bacteria itself</u> (adult botulinum is caused by ingesting the toxin).
-<u>Botulinum</u> has a **descending** paralysis. In infants, give <u>human-derived anti-toxin &</u> <u>supportive care</u>.

-<u>Heat exhaustion</u> is <40C/105F <u>without CNS symptoms</u>, and is <u>due to volume depletion</u> (like sweating too much). (It 'can' lead to <u>Heat stroke</u> (>105 + CNS symptoms) which is due to failure of the thermoregulatory center).

-Don't forget that <u>Waterhouse-Friderichsen</u> is due to DIC and is **fatal**! (<u>more common in</u> <u>children</u>)

-<u>Bloody stool and Eosinophils</u> in Neonates, suspect <u>Milk protein intolerance</u>! (or any food allergy!)

-Conduction hearing loss in a kid...think <u>Eustachian tube defect</u>! Kid will complain of fullness in the ear, audible pop when swallowing. <u>Usually presents post-URTI</u>. On otoscopy look for decreased retraction/mobility of the tympanic membrane. Also <u>characteristic here is middle ear effusion</u>. (**Just keep in mind that Otitis can also cause conduction hearing loss...and so we can differentiate this with Otitis cuz this is Afebrile!)

-Heparin can cause <u>thrombosis</u>! (<u>via Ab-mediated platelet activation</u>)

-Increased <u>b-hCG, think Choriocarcinoma</u>. Increased <u>a-FP, think Yolk Sac/Endodermal</u> <u>sinus tumor</u>.

-Pain, redness, sweating, and swelling (but afebrile)...consider "<u>Reflex Sympathetic</u>

Dystrophy" (aka Sudeck's atrophy!). This is pain following injury to bone or soft tissue, hence usually caused by direct trauma, or sometimes even MI!
-We see here muscle spasms, affected skin, affected bones. Treat with Physical Therapy, or Steroids in resistant cases.

-Osteopenia is a decrease in bone mass (often a precursor to Osteoporosis, also often seen in young female athletes, along with amenorrhea & eating disorders seen in young female athletes).
(Recall that Osteopenia was also seen in Reflex Sympathetic Dystrophy)

-Most sensitive for diagnosing Osteoporosis is Quantitative CT. (Gold standard is spine & pelvis **DEXA**)

-Increased osteoid deposition, think Vitamin D deficiency. (I know, kinda counter-intuitive!)

-Paget's, not just big head, also **decreased hearing** (due to bone formation around CN8).
-Recall most patients with Paget's are asymptomatic and need no treatment.
(Only treat those with symptoms)

-Urinary n-Telopeptide & Deoxypyridinoline can be used as markers of bone resorption.

-Abundant mineralization of periosteum, think too much Vitamin A.

-Metformin's lactic acidosis is worst in patients with Renal Failure.
(So in any renal failure patient…watch out when giving Metformin)

-Adrenal insufficiency, don't forget to consider things like Autoimmune adrenalitis, or Adrenal TB…or also cessation of steroid meds.
(Recall we confirm adrenal insufficiency with ACTH stimulation test. Cortisol >20 excludes insufficiency!)
(In the acute steroid cessation adrenal insufficiency, look for abd pain, hypoglycemia, & hypotension. Here Aldosterone levels are NORMAL, so patient will be **Normokalemic**)

-Optic glioma (slowly progressive unilateral visual loss & dyschromatopsia (problems with color perception)), and Iris hamartoma (so-called Lisch nodules)…think **Neurofibromatosis**!

-Retinal Hamartoma (instead of Iris hamartoma), Angiofibromas, seizures, heart rhabdo…think Tuberous sclerosis.

-The Dystonia seen with the Extrapyramidal side-effects of anti-psychotics can include Opisthotonus. (So don't think C. Tetanus as soon as you see Opisthotonus!) (can even be seen in Lithium tox)

-Asbestos can cause both Mesothelioma AND Bronchogenic carcinoma (which is actually more common than Mesothelioma). And both can have pleural plaques.

-For Syphilis...**Pen, Tetra, Z**. (When diagnosing it, just remember that VDRL may be negative in the initial stages. So instead do dark-field microscopy.

-For ascites, after doing a diagnostic paracentesis, start empiric therapy (3rd Cephalo), just in case there is a bacterial peritonitis.

-If it has **>250 PMN's**, then we have ourselves a bacterial peritonitis. (Note that we won't necessarily see leukocytosis in the blood in bacterial peritonitis)

(With confirmed bacterial peritonitis, Tx with Quinolones or 3rd Cephalo, to cover Gram-negative)

-Recall that **Serum – Albumin less than 1** can be Nephrotic Syndrome, TB, or Cancer (Just know that Ascites can be severe enough to cause pulmonary distress!)

-For Croup (viral), give Cool mist, Steroids, Racemic Epi.

-For Epiglottitis (bacterial), bring to OR, endotracheal/oral intubation or tracheostomy, & iv antibiotics.

-Decreased perfusion can cause both Prerenal AND Renal (ATN) failure.

-Prerenal, look for **Urine Na <20 & FeNa <1** (cuz reabsorbing Na and not filtering well)

(Renal (ATN), look for Urine Na >20 & FeNa >2 (cuz can't reabsorb Na))

(FeNa can be calculated by U_{Na} x P_{Cr} / U_{Cr} x P_{Na})

-Good idea to order U/S on patients with Acute RF, to r/o post-renal cause!

-ATN...look for Mud-Brown/Granular casts & Renal tubular cells

-In Sideroblastic anemia (one of the causes of microcytic anemia (along with thalassemia & Iron-deficiency), you get elevated everything! (elevated Serum Iron, Ferritin, and TIBC)

-Decreased platelet count & recurrent arterial/venous thrombosis...think Anti-phospholipid Ab. There are 3 types of this: **FP Syphilis** (recall FP VDRL is also seen in Erythema Nodosum), **Lupus anticoagulant** (falsely elevates PTT), **Anti-cardiolipin Ab**.

-Anti-phospholipid Ab doesn't always present with SLE.

-For Pseudo, give 4th Cephalo (fepime, taz), Pipera/Ticar, Aminoglycs, or Quinolones.

-A long-term complication of Lyme disease includes Lyme arthritis (joint pains, swelling, restricted ROM)

-If bitten by tick, but no rash and no symptoms...no need for prophylactic antibiotics EXCEPT in pregnancy, where it's recommended to give prophylactic Amox.

-Recall for Lyme disease, give Doxy, because it also covers Ehrlichia (EXCEPT kids/pregnancy, then give Amox)

CHAPTER 8.

How to Review

The last two chapters were spent focusing on the importance of taking notes, from both your books as well as from the practice questions you have been doing. When it comes down to reviewing those notes, keep the following things in mind:

- Be dynamic

- Condense

- Cross-reference

Be dynamic

Whether it is adding a little drawing, including arrows, re-organizing the contents, or adding or deleting info, there are a few reasons why you should change your notes as you review them. The most significant reason is that changing your notes as you review resolves the monotony of reviewing. No one likes to review, but by deciding to change things around, you are already getting yourself more involved in your notes, as opposed to just reading and memorizing them. You are deciding if what you previously wrote makes sense, if it is written clearly, if the order is in a logical manner, if there are things you could add to the side, if there are charts or diagrams you could add, and if there are images or drawings you can add, etc.

Get actively involved with your notes as you review them. Constantly update them, with the aim of perfecting them. Every time you review your notes, you want it to feel new and fresh. The ideal note is one that takes a dull topic, and makes it fun and appealing. It is visually attractive, yet easy on the eyes. It is condensed, yet resourceful. Some of my favorite things to do in my notes as you may have noticed are to change the font styles around, like making some lines *italic*, some lines **bold**, and some underlined. I put some things in (brackets), and preceded some things by → arrows. For really important things I would make the font larger, or write it in a different color. Sometimes I even wrote myself little notes, such as, "I know you hate learning about this topic, but the following is a possible test question, so just memorize it!" I put *** before important things that should not be forgotten, etc.

Remember, it is you who will need to keep reviewing your notes again and again. You are only improving your notes for yourself. Make the effort to perfect your notes to your liking, in a way that would improve the arduous task of reviewing.

Condense your notes

Condense your notes from time to time. By reviewing it every so often you start becoming familiar with some of it. Instead of going over everything, every time you review, keep condensing your notes, by removing material that you are certain you're familiar with, and that you know you will remember in weeks to come.

This is how I condensed the *First Aid* into twenty-seven pages of notes. The first time around it was closer to fifty or so pages. Then as I kept reviewing my notes, there were some topics that just became stuck in my mind and that I knew I was comfortable with. I therefore re-wrote my notes, leaving all that redundant information out, so that every subsequent time I reviewed, I would be spending my time efficiently, and only reviewing pertinent information that I knew I needed to review.

This is where it helps to type notes. It makes this process a lot easier. Although if your notes are written, and you condense your notes by re-writing them, the act of writing itself helps you retain the information.

Cross-reference

Probably the most important thing you need to do when you review your notes is to cross-reference the information. This is paramount in succeeding in USMLE-style questions. What I mean by cross-referencing is that when you run into a disease that sounds familiar for example, try to find where you have seen it before (again here is where it helps to have typed notes, because you can use a word processor's "find word" option). When you do find where you saw it mentioned before, put that in your notes!

With the Wegner's Granulomatosis example in the "Randomize" section of Chapter 4 (Set Up a Schedule), what you should be doing is adding a little side note in your renal pathology notes that mentions that it also affects the lungs, and adding a little side note in your pulmonary pathology notes that mentions how it also affects the kidneys.

Or, for example, in one of your reviewing sessions, you read about Hepatitis C in your microbiology notes, and read that it has some association with Porphyria Cutanea Tarda as well as Lymphomas. You do not think much of it at the time, but at some future date, you start reviewing your biochemistry notes, and heme synthesis to be specific, and run into Porphyria Cutanea Tarda, and suddenly you remember that you read about it somewhere before.

It is not just enough to make that faint recall. Find out exactly where you saw it, and read that section from your previous notes. Then put a little note on the side of your biochemistry notes, saying, "Remember that Hepatitis C has some association with Porphyria Cutanea Tarda." Similarly, at some future date when you are reviewing your pathology notes and run into Lymphoma, again you remember seeing it somewhere. Go back and find it in your microbiology notes under Hepatitis C. Make sure to add a side note that says how Hepatitis C is associated with Lymphoma.

Once you start getting into the habit of doing this, go even further, and in your Lymphoma notes for example, write, "Hepatitis C is associated with Lymphoma as well as Porphyria Cutanea Tarda (PTC). Remember that PTC is a deficiency in the fifth step of Heme synthesis."

In your biochemistry notes

Remember that Hepatitis C is associated With Porphyria Cutanea Tarda (recall that HepC is also associated with Lymphoma)-	**- Porphyria Cutanea Tarda is an enzyme deficiency in heme synthesis** **- Symptoms of PTC include photosensitivity...**

In your pathology notes:

Recall that Hepatitis C is associated with Lymphomas, as well as with Porphyria Cutanea Tarda (recall that PTC is a deficiency in a Heme synthesis enzyme...	**- Lymphomas are neoplasms that originate from lymphocytes** **- There are 2 main types, Hodgkin's & Non-Hodgkin's . . .**

Do you realize how you are slowly combining information from every subject with one another? You are now prepping yourself for those second and third order USMLE questions. Such that if the question presents a patient with Lymphoma, you remember from your notes that Lymphoma can be associated with Hepatitic C, and Hepatitis C can be associated with Porphyria Cutanea Tarda, and Porphyria Cutanea Tarda is a problem with Heme synthesis. Those higher order questions are that easy if you know *how* to review your notes.

Getting into the habit of doing this will cover all grounds, such that you cover the USMLE questions from all angles. Remember, those questions love to incorporate different subjects into one question stem, and if you know all the associations, it will make questions that much easier.

Always make every effort to find out where you saw a disease, symptom, or treatment, even if it sounds just faintly familiar. If you think you read it somewhere before, odds are you have. Find out where, and put a note in both your old notes where you first saw it, as well as in your new notes where you just saw it again. Always cross-reference. You will be surprised how effective this is.

If you look at my sample notes, you will notice that they are full of cross-references. Every line in my notes that begins with "Remember that this is" or "Recall that we saw this in" is a cross-reference.

CHAPTER 9.

Aim High

I recall one of my colleagues in medical school, who was an average student, once telling me, "All I want is an 85. I'd be happy with that."

His comment baffled me. I did not then, and still do not understand how anyone could say something like that. It is one thing to be realistic and to know what score you are likely to get, but it is another thing to sell yourself short and to start your USMLE prep already convinced that you are limited in your success. If you think that way, then odds are you will most likely do poorly on the exam.

No matter where you stand, there is absolutely nothing wrong with aiming for the top and setting ninety-nine as your goal. If you do not have that top score to aim for, you will not achieve it. It is as simple as that. Convince yourself from day one that you will aim for and receive a ninety-nine. Always aim high, and never sell yourself short. Never question your abilities to do well. Doing well is a function of dedication, discipline, and drive. Set ninety-nine as your goal and aim for it. Your chances of getting it will be a lot higher if you do.

* * *

Never decide to "take the hit" on any subject or topic. Do you see the irony in that statement? Just by saying you will take the hit on something you are admitting that you are lacking in that certain subject/topic! You should be grateful that you know what you need to work on, and instead of "taking the hit," work on strengthening that particular subject/topic. The problem most test-takers face is that they do not know where they need work. If you already know where you are weak, you are one step ahead of most other test-takers.

Remember, every question on the USMLEs counts, and theoretically, your aim is to get every single question right. That is the mentality that you need, not only going into the test, but also when you study. Therefore, do not neglect any topics. Each time you do, think of it as one question that you will be incapable of answering during the exam. Looking at it another way, think of it as one step closer to failing.

CHAPTER 10.

Take Practice Exams

Remember that an excellent way of knowing where you stand when you first start your USMLE prep is to take a practice NBME test. It gives you a realistic idea of the score you would likely receive, and it gives you a very useful performance profile to help you tweak your study habits. It is a fantastic way of planning your USMLE prep.

Now you have started your preparation, and it has been a few weeks since you started studying. How do you make sure you are on the right track? How do you make sure you are progressing? Is it just a matter of feeling more confident? Is it just a matter of getting better and better scores on question books and question banks?

It's actually a combination of factors that you should take into account to monitor your progress (remember those questions in Chapter One that you should be asking yourself from time to time?). Your confidence, your knowledge, and your scores on question books and question banks are a great way of assessing your progress over the long-term, but no question bank out there will accurately portray your expected USMLE score the way the practice NBME exams do. The grade you receive on NBME practice exams is the closest predictor of your expected USMLE score (though this is not a guarantee and is in no way advertised as such by the NBME). However, it is known as such from experience. In fact, the NBME I took one week before my Step 1 was only one point below my actual USMLE score, and all my colleagues had similar experiences. Do not take my word for it though. Ask any senior you know who has taken an NBME practice test within a week of their USMLE. You will notice how eerily accurate the NBME practice tests are at predicting your USMLE score.

* * *

To make sure you are on the right track, to get an accurate picture of where you stand, and an accurate representation of your progress, take NBME practice exams throughout your study schedule. For example, if you are giving yourself eight weeks to study, take an NBME on day one, in week three, in week five, and in week seven (remember, there are four different ones available on the NBME web site).

Doing so will be an eye-opener. You will see where you stand, and where your strong/weak points are, but most importantly of all, you will see if you are improving. This is crucial during this valuable time spent studying for the USMLE.

If you notice your scores are low, then the first thing you should do is be grateful you took an NBME practice exam! It is better to know early where you really stand, rather than knowing later on. If such is the case, then clearly there is something not working in your studies. Perhaps, as the performance profile might clearly show, you are not working hard enough on your weak subjects. Perhaps the knowledge base is there, but you simply need to do more practice questions. Maybe you have just been using the wrong books thus far. Whatever it is, knowing where you stand allows you to adjust your study plan and/or schedule accordingly, and re-direct yourself to the right track.

If you take an NBME practice exam halfway through your studies and realize you are not doing well, don't lose your cool. Be grateful. Use this newfound information to your advantage. Figure out what is going wrong and fix it. Use your poor score to motivate you to work even harder.

If, on the other hand, you notice your scores are indeed improving and/or are high, do not get too excited just yet. Remember, there is always room for improvement. Do not just settle with a satisfying level of progress, but rather aim even higher! Work on those weaker subjects and fine-tune those test-taking skills. You can never work too hard. Use your good score to motivate you to go even further. Clearly, you are on the right track, so now just spend that extra effort and aim for that ninety-nine.

CHAPTER 11.

Know Your Enemy

Ever heard the saying, "Knowing is half the battle," or "Know your enemy" (from Sun Tzu's *The Art of War*)?

One of the biggest factors affecting your USMLE score is your stress level. No matter how much you study, and how much you think you know, if you are nervous the day of the test, you will do horribly. There is simply no way around it. Do not expect your intelligence or your many hours of studying to come into play. Being nervous physiologically affects your thinking in a negative way.

Luckily though, there is a way to appease at least some of that predicted nervousness—know the exam. Get to know everything about it—where it is, how to drive there, how long it takes to get there, the whole process once you enter the test center, the room you will be in, how many questions there are, how many hours it is, the computer program it's on, what you will have for lunch, where the bathrooms are, what you will have in your locker, and what you will be wearing. Know everything.

In the months and weeks prior to your exam, visualize yourself taking the exam. Visualize how calm and relaxed you are. Visualize yourself answering the questions correctly and confidently. Visualize the whole day from the moment you wake up, to the moment you are at the test center, to the moment you complete the exam. Daydream about it from time to time, and think about it as you are falling asleep every night. Make a routine of doing so.

It will help you stay calm and relaxed during the exam, as you will know exactly what to expect. You will not be out of your comfort zone, since you have visualized yourself going through the whole process hundreds of times by now. You will be comfortable and unperturbed.

As soon as you know at which test center you will be taking your test, go visit it. In fact, unless it has changed, the USMLE allows you to take a practice exam at an official test center for a small fee (information is on their web site). This is a great way of getting familiar with your test center, as it will allow you to physically go through the whole process of taking a test at one of their test centers, as opposed to just visualizing yourself doing it!

CHAPTER 12.

Test-Taking Skills

There are hundreds of books out there on test-taking skills, so I will only add a few tips that I feel might be helpful.

Basics

I think the section regarding test-taking in Kaplan®'s question book is fair. It covers basics such as the different types of questions, different ways to approach a question, and so on. I will however stress the importance of reading the actual question (usually the last sentence in the stem), before reading the stem. Doing so will help you look for clues as you read the stem. In the limited amount of time that you have, when you read a paragraph-long stem, you want to know what you are looking for.

For example, if the question is asking you to pick the bacteria responsible for a patient's illness, then the past medical and family history might not be so important to you. You may therefore be able to skip that section of the stem. Or if the question asks you to manage someone's chest pain, then the fact that the patient was camping two weeks ago and ate raw meat may not affect your answer very much. The USMLE is full of these questions, where the stem gives you a lot of clues and information, many of which have nothing to do with the question that is finally asked.

Read the question first so that you know what you are looking for when you read the stem. Sometimes I feel like these stems are written in a way to purposely steer you in one direction and make you think of one thing, only to completely surprise you at the end of the stem, and steer the question in a completely different direction.

Lastly, regarding basics, one thing that is commonly overlooked (admittedly even by myself), is to read the stem in FULL. Often the deciding clue will be the last line of the stem, right before the question. I have seen this all too many times, and luckily caught it numerous times. The test writers know that many readers will come up with an answer halfway through reading the stem based on some of the clues presented, and will pick an answer and move on. More often than not, you will get the correct answer and will not miss anything by skipping the remainder of the stem if you feel there are enough clues to support your answer. However, the few times that there are more clues near the end of the stem, you do not want to miss them. Every question counts and you do not want to miss easy questions just because you did not read the stem in full.

Association

There are tons of clues in any given question stem, and it is up to you to pick them up. These include age, sex, location, symptoms, medications, family history, and past medical history, etc.

Do not overlook these clues. They are often there for a reason. In fact, this is why you practice doing questions! You need to start training yourself to associate these clues with crucial information that may help you answer the question. For example:

When you see an elderly patient, right away start thinking of:

> -diverticulitis
> -multidrug therapy
> -dementia
> -pneumonia

When you see a young patient, start thinking of:

> -AML
> -congenital diseases
> -viral infections

When you see a teen or young adult patient, start thinking of:

> -Infectious Mononucleosis

-Gonorrhea

-Anorexia

In terms of locations, the following are examples of associations:

- If you see Southeast Asia, think TB, Malaria

- If you see Caribbean, think Hepatitis A, E. Coli, Salmonella

- If you see Africa, think Sickle Cell, Malaria, G6PDH deficiency

In terms of past medical history, the following are examples of associations:

- If you see hypercholesterolemia, think rhabdomyolysis from Statins

- If you see rheumatoid arthritis, think renal toxicity from NSAID use

- If you see diabetes mellitus, think lactic acidosis from Metformin

There is an ever-ending list of other associations that you should start to make, such as:

- If you see any southwestern state, think Coccidioides

- If there is mention of water, think Legionella, Leptospira

- If there is mention of camping, think Giardia, Lyme disease

- If patient is immunosuppressed, think CMV, Cryptosporidium, HSV, TB, HIV

- If patient has renal toxicity, think Aspirin

- And so on...

These associations are tools you should practice using as you read the question stem. As soon as you hit a word or clue in the stem, start making associations right away. It helps you think of a diagnosis as you are reading the question stem, and it helps you think "outside the box," so that instead of just reading the question and taking it for what it's worth, you are considering everything that revolves around the patient. This helps because as you know, USMLE questions are rarely ever first-order questions. They are often second- or third-order questions. Training yourself to start making these associations as you read a question stem will help you make sense of those "tough" USMLE questions.

Either you know it or you don't

If you do not know the answer right away, do not waste your time. The answer will not come to you if you just keep reading the question again and again, or if you stare at the answer options. Either you know the answer or you don't. By wasting time on a question you are not sure about, you're losing time you could be using on other questions that you are sure about. So if you do not know the answer, just make an educated guess and move on, do not lag. You can mark it, and return to it later if you have time.

Remember to stay calm if you do not know the answer. There is absolutely no shame in it. You are not expected to know the answer to every single question. Just try your best, pick the answer option that best fits, and move on.

CHAPTER 13.

Last Advice

There was a study done where a group of similar aged and similar intellectual-leveled children were split into two groups right before they were about to take the exact same test. One group was told before the test that they were the smarter of the two groups, whereas the other group was told before the test that they were the dumber of the two groups.

Even though both groups were on average the same intellectually, the group that was told they were smarter scored on average much higher on the same test, as the group that was told they were intellectually inferior.

What does that mean for you, the reader? It's quite simple.

- Never put yourself down

- Always compliment yourself

- Convince yourself you are smart

- Convince yourself you are smarter than all other USMLE test takers

- Convince yourself you will succeed on the USMLEs effortlessly

I want all of you to write the following on a piece of paper:

I am the smartest.

People named (your name) are the smartest.

I will get 99 on the USMLE™.

I will answer every question correctly.

There is nothing that I don't know.

I know the correct answer and I will pick it every time.

The USMLEs™ are very easy for me.

I am extremely confident.

I will get 99.

I am the smartest.

Read the above every morning when you wake up, and every night before going to sleep. Cherish it. Believe it.

The day of the test, write down the following on the laminated sheet you get:

I am the smartest.

I will answer every question correctly.

I will get 99.

This has been studied to work. I do it myself before every test, and I have no doubt that it works on a subconscious level in increasing the level of confidence, and decreasing the level of nervousness. Give it a shot.

With that said, I wish you the best of luck. I know you will all do just fine. I realize that the weeks leading to the USMLE are the most miserable weeks of your life, but you can get through it, like so many have done so already. Just be confident, stay motivated, and keep working hard.

Armin Kamyab, M.D.

As with my first book, *How to Study in Medical School*, my sole intention in writing this book is to help you triumph over the USMLEs. As such, all comments and suggestions are gladly welcome, as they would only help improve future editions.

arminkamyab@gmail.com

Notes

Notes

Notes

Armin Kamyab, M.D., is currently a General Surgery resident. He tutored extensively through all four years of medical school covering every subject, from first year biochemistry and histology to second year pathology and microbiology. Dr. Kamyab is  known at his medical school campus not only for his great love for teaching and helping his colleagues, but more importantly for his ability to effortlessly absorb the wealth of information presented, as well as his uncanny ability to conquer all examinations, including the standardized licensing examinations.

Printed in the United Kingdom by
Lightning Source UK Ltd., Milton Keynes
141262UK00001B/33/P